The CUP
and the
WATERFALL

The CUP
and the
WATERFALL

*The Adventure of Living in the
Present Moment*

JOHN KILLINGER

PAULIST PRESS
New York/Ramsey

Library of Congress
Catalog Card Number: 82-61421

ISBN: 0-8091-2515-3

Published by Paulist Press
545 Island Road, Ramsey, N.J. 07446

Printed and bound in the
United States of America

Contents

Continuously renewed immediacy, not receding memory of the Divine Touch, lies at the base of religious living.

Thomas Kelly
A Testament of Devotion

The Cup and the Waterfall

A friend of mine was changing planes in the old Atlanta airport. It was late in the afternoon, and the corridors were crowded with people going to and from their planes. Many were tired, and their faces reflected the tensions of a long day. Tempers were edgy as they hurried along, trying to make connections or get to taxicabs.

Coming toward her in the crowd, my friend saw an elderly lady being pushed in a wheelchair by a younger companion. Suddenly, as they were almost abreast of one another, the elderly lady exclaimed, in a voice loud enough for everyone to hear, "Good work, God!"

Nearly everyone in the corridor turned to look at the old lady, and saw that she was looking out the windows of the corridor. Their eyes followed hers, and saw a majestic sunset lighting up the sky.

Smiles broke out on all the faces.

Shoulders were squared and thrown back.

Steps were lighter.

The atmosphere of the entire place was transformed by the elderly lady's eye and observation.

"Good work, God."

Indeed it was—and is.

What a matchless world we live in! A world of sunsets, books, candles, stars, and apple orchards . . . of mountains and meadows and church spires . . . of children and pine trees and singing brooks and cloudless skies . . . of wood fires and snowfalls and pollywogs and caterpillars . . . of old shoes and heavy sweaters and warm soups and porcelain coffee cups.

It is a world thick with the presence of God, with evidences of his loving care on every hand.

It isn't any wonder that the psalmist said his cup was overflowing, or that Annie Dillard, a modern psalmist of another kind, described grace as a waterfall, and us with our cups down under it, trying to catch it in its superabundance.

Our only problem, as Dillard saw, is that we can't catch enough because our cups are always full.

"Experiencing the present purely," she said, "is being emptied and hollow; you catch grace as a man fills his cup under a waterfall."[1]

Much of it we fail to experience because we are like the people in the airport corridor; our lives are filled with other things—with appointments, dreams, goals, desires, memories, the stuff of other places and

1. *Pilgrim at Tinker Creek* (New York: Harper's Magazine Press, 1974), pp. 80–81.

other times. We miss the here and now for the there and then.

To experience the present—the world in all its glory—we have to be emptied and hollow. Or, in the words of another woman writer, we have to lie open and waiting, the way a beach lies open for a gift from the sea.[2]

That is the catch.

To experience the world, one must be receptive. One must be alert, as the old woman in the wheelchair was. Otherwise, one misses everything.

I remember a minister who used to pray in the invocation, "You could not be here more truly, Lord, but we could."

And a woman I saw buying a carton of cigarettes one Sunday morning in Massachusetts, saying to the girl behind the counter, "There's nothing to do around here on Sunday but smoke."

Nothing to do but smoke—in the country of Thoreau, who studied for hours the shifting currents and shadows of Walden Pond, and Bronson Alcott, who founded a school for transcendental thinking, and George Lyman Kittridge, the famous Shakespeare scholar who never earned a doctor's degree because there was no one smart or learned enough to give him an examination.

She wasn't looking out the window, was she? The world was full of the glory of God, and all she knew to do was smoke.

---

2. Anne Morrow Lindbergh, *Gift from the Sea* (New York: Pantheon Press, 1955), p. 17.

I think of another woman I have known. She was a victim of arthritis. And she was poor. She lived in one room, never going out for years except to the bathroom and, when she was able to make the trip, to the dining room for a bit of food.

Yet there was a richness to her life in that one room you wouldn't believe.

She treasured little things—little notes from friends, little clippings from papers and church bulletins, little songs of birds outside her window, little Christmas decorations she hung on a battered little artificial tree. She was invariably cheerful when you went to see her. She treasured visits, among other things.

There, in her room, with her gnarled and painful hands, she held her cup under the waterfall.

And it was so empty it was always being filled.

The ancient mystics understood this, and tried to make a rule for living this way all the time. Some of them called it "entering the void"; others, "blanking the mind"; still others, "annihilating the self."

They learned that, to the extent that we are able to eliminate desire and concentrate on the wonders passing before our eyes, we experience the world as the theater of God.

By giving up our claim on everything, we discover a richness beyond all our dreams.

By renouncing ownership, we own everything— or enjoy its use, which is just as good.

Then we are freed to pray—to participate in God, as they would say.

To be part of the miracle. To be one with God in Christ.

We even pray, I think, by being grateful for the world we live in. By seeing the waterfall, and giving thanks for our cups.

It isn't a matter of being in church. Church is part of the waterfall, like the rest of the world.

It is a matter of being aware, and being thankful, wherever you are.

There is a passage in a book by Marcus Bach, a wonderfully worldly man in the best sense of that word, about his boyhood in Wisconsin. It was one of those bright, limpid spring days when Wisconsin was being transformed from a winter wasteland to a warm, almost summer wonderland. And it was the first day of the fishing season.

Unfortunately, it was also a Sunday.

In the little German community where the Bachs lived, Sundays were reserved for church. There was never any question about it.

Except on this particular Sunday.

Marcus' father, normally a devout churchgoer, announced that he was going fishing and intended to take the boy with him. He had worked hard in his store all week, and wanted to be outdoors.

The mother was scandalized. What would people say?

The father didn't care; he was going fishing.

All right, the mother finally said, but not with the boy. The boy must go to church.

With the boy too, the father said.

And soon they were pedaling their bikes the four miles out to the old mill where the fish would be.

It was a beautiful day and excitement was electric in the air. But Marcus felt guilty. God wouldn't like him to be fishing on the sabbath.

As if to underscore his feelings, they pedaled past a graveyard. The gravestones—gruesome, weather-beaten old markers—were God's trump card. Father and son might go fishing on the sabbath, but God would get them in the end. No one escaped the wrath. The trip was almost spoiled.

Then Marcus realized something, and a sense of victory surged through him. He realized that God liked fishing.

"God liked fishing. Jesus liked fishermen. God liked this Sunday-morning world."[3]

God's world was the open road and the fields of new-growing corn along the way. God's world was a father and son riding their bicycles out to the old mill to go fishing. God's world included the people going to church and the people going fishing, as long as they all loved the Lord.

At the mill, father and son laid their bicycles in deep grass and made their way silently to the edges of the dark pool.

Green flakes of algae covered the water. Lily pads shimmered in the sunlight. Beds of watercress grew softly at their feet, and the green hills rose beyond the mill.

3. Marcus Bach, *The Power of Perception* (New York: Hawthorn Books, 1965), p. 135.

Standing and smelling the fresh scent of willow trees, the boy thought his heart would burst. An old church song sprang unbidden in his mind:

Come thou Almighty King,
Help us thy name to sing,
Help us to praise,
Father all glorious,
O'er all victorious,
Come and reign over us,
Ancient of days.

The world was a waterfall, and his young mind was a cup trying to catch it. As an older man, he could say with the psalmist, "My cup runneth over." It always does, if only we have eyes to see.

The important thing is to be emptied and hollow, not filled with other things.

To have time to meditate on the goodness of God.

To see the sunsets that transform our corridors.

Then we too will say "Good work, God," and hold our cups under the waterfall.

✝ ✝ ✝

PRAYER

O God, who art known in sunrise and sunset, in the green of springtime and the sear of autumn, in the breaking of bread and the groaning of the board, we praise your name for the splendor of grace. Let us give thanks by using all things in moderation, and by keeping our cups empty, ready for the waterfall. For yours is the bountiful kingdom, now and forever. Amen.

7

Now about eight days after these sayings he took with him Peter and John and James, and went up on the mountain to pray. And as he was praying, the appearance of his countenance was altered, and his raiment became dazzling white. And behold, two men talked with him, Moses and Elijah, who appeared in glory and spoke of his departure, which he was to accomplish at Jerusalem. Now Peter and those who were with him were heavy with sleep but kept awake, and they saw his glory and the two men who stood with him.

And as the men were parting from him, Peter said to Jesus, "Master, it is well that we are here; let us make three booths, one for you and one for Moses and one for Elijah"—not knowing what he said. As he said this, a cloud came and overshadowed them; and they were afraid as they entered the cloud. And a voice came out of the cloud, saying, "This is my Son, my Chosen; listen to him!" And when the voice had spoken, Jesus was found alone. And they kept silence and told no one in those days anything of what they had seen.

Luke 9:28–36 (RSV)

The facts of mental ability already discovered in parapsychology no more fit the current idea of a space-time world than such a fact that ships disappear bottom-first over the horizon fits the model of a flat earth.

Louisa Rhine
Journal of Parapsychology

Living only in the visible world is living on the surface; it ignores or sets aside not only the existence of God but the depths of created being. It is condemning ourselves to perceiving only the world's surface.

Anthony Bloom
Courage To Pray

The cross is a heart-breaker; the empty tomb is a mind-breaker. Both heart and mind need to be broken.

Chad Walsh
God at Large

Prayer and the Resurrection

Several years ago I received a letter from a young woman I had met in Guatemala. She was from a lovely Christian family. Her father owned a chain of hotels through Central and South America. She had been an airline stewardess, but, when I met her, she was studying hotel management, intending to work for her father.

The letter came to apprise me of a tragedy in the family. Her younger brother, who was sixteen, had driven his little sports car into the mountains above Guatemala City. There he had been murdered, apparently by some poor creatures who wanted only to steal the tires from his car. The police had never found the murderers.

"I am not bitter," wrote the young woman, "and I have not spoken against God. I understand that these things happen. But I want to know one thing. What about the resurrection?"

What about the resurrection?

How would you have answered her?

I spent several days composing an answer, and tore up more than one letter. The letter I finally sent still did not satisfy me, and I continued to draft answers in my head. At last, months later, I realized what I should have said.

I should have said, "My dear, you cannot understand the resurrection without prayer."

Let me explain.

We live in a very hard-facts kind of world. Our orientation is largely scientific and rationalistic. In such a world, the idea of the resurrection, of a life beyond our day-to-day existence, is incomprehensible. You may recall the redoubtable old man of English letters, Dr. Samuel Johnson, and his quarrel with Bishop Berkeley, the philosophical idealist. Dr. Johnson kicked a stone, injuring his foot, and said, "Thus I refute Berkeley!" There is something of that hardheaded realism about all of us. Our world breeds it.

When my young friend in Guatemala wrote to me and asked about the resurrection, my answer had to swim against the current of everyday realism. And I made the mistake of trying to give it water wings and help it to do so. I attempted to explain, from Scripture and from common sense, how the resurrection could be true. What I should have done—what I failed to do— was to talk about prayer as a way of entering the experience of resurrection, so that my friend would have *known* the resurrection and would not have needed it explained.

Prayer, you see, is the Christian's way of perceiving the irrational, of going beyond the facticity of the everyday world and apprehending with an inner eye the reality of transcendental existence.

This, I think, is the primary significance of the story of Jesus' transfiguration on the mountain. Jesus and the disciples were in prayer. They had been on the mountain for hours, perhaps even days, and had been praying the whole time. And that night, when fatigue had descended upon them, the disciples saw something that nearly made their eyes pop out: Jesus was transformed into an ethereal being, his body and clothing dazzling with light, and was talking with Moses and Elijah, the two most popular figures in Hebrew history.

They had simply prayed to the point where they could see into the spiritual nature of things, and where the line between the ordinary world and the spiritual world was obliterated.

Now, that such a world of spiritual things exists is posited by many experiences outside the boundaries of Christian theology or practice.

For example, there is the evidence of ESP and PK—extrasensory perception and psychokinesis—the extraordinary ability, verified by empirical science, that some people have to send and receive communications through space and time, to dream clairvoyant dreams, and to produce physical effects in inert materials without touching them. Uri Geller, perhaps the best known psychic in the world, has repeatedly demonstrated that he can bend keys and spoons and other metal objects merely by concentrating his thought upon them, and is even reported to have done so over television, bending objects in people's homes who were watching him on their sets. We don't understand such power. It defies what we know about the universe. But scientists have examined Geller at work and say that he really does change the shape of objects without touching them.

There is strange evidence too of something called the transmigration of souls—of people being inhabited by the souls of other persons already dead. There is a woman in Virginia, for example—a Methodist minister's wife. Her husband used hypnosis on her to ease her terrible migraine headaches, and under hypnosis she began to speak in fluent German, though she had never learned a word of German in her life. In German, she described in perfect detail a small German village she had never seen. Tom Brokaw, who was then a young mobile reporter for NBC, came down to interview her, and returned to New York shaken by the experience. "I have seen many frauds in my time," he said, "but that woman is no fraud."

Then there is the story of Arigo, the Brazilian social worker with extraordinary powers of healing. For several years before his death in 1973, this heavy-set man who looked like a truck driver or a farm worker would go into a trance and begin to work medical wonders under the influence of a German doctor who supposedly had died years before and had sworn to make up in his afterlife for a lack of medical competence during his ordinary lifetime. American author John Fuller went to South America and wrote a book about him. Doctors from all over the world came there to see him. He simply stood patients up against the wall, immediately diagnosed their problems, and treated them instantly. He wrote advanced pharmaco-logical prescriptions, though he had never had a lesson in pharmaceutics. He performed delicate operations with a mere penknife or a kitchen knife, without even anesthetizing the patients, and they felt no pain and did not bleed more than a drop of blood.[1]

How do we explain such things? We can't—not in any scientific fashion. Nor are these isolated occur-rences. There are many similar tales.

And while we are near the subject, what do you make of the thousands of reports of "life after life" we have heard or read since Elisabeth Kübler-Ross first published her book *On Death and Dying?*

One of my students related to me this strange in-cident: His small son fell into a swimming pool when no one was looking, and was discovered floating face down in the water. There was no pulse, and his body had turned blue. Frantic efforts at resuscitation finally brought the child back to life. When he was able to speak, he said that he had been with "Franklin." His parents looked at each other in amazement; Franklin was the name of his grandfather, whom he had never seen or heard called by that name. Somehow, in the marginal area between this world and the next, the boy had become acquainted with a man who had died before he was born!

A woman in Texas told me this story that held such meaning for her sister who was dying of cancer. It was of a well known woman in California who, as

1. John G. Fuller, *Arigo: Surgeon of the Rusty Knife* (New York: Thomas Y. Crowell, 1974).

she slipped away from life, began calling out from her bed to dead acquaintances she was greeting in the other life. Among the persons she greeted was a cousin whose death notice did not reach the family in California until two weeks after the woman died! She had no earthly way of knowing the cousin had died—no *earthly* way.

There it is: the irrational world that borders on our everyday world, that invades it from time to time, that shatters its pretensions of being the most ultimately real world there is.

We can't explain it.

We only glimpse it occasionally.

We cannot hold it.

It is in no way orthodox, or amenable to traditional doctrine.

But prayer is a door into this world.

I am not speaking, of course, of the discrete little prayers we offer on specific occasions. I am talking about prayer as a way of life, prayer as frequent meditation, prayer as constant openness to God, prayer as waiting before God until God discloses his spirit to the one praying, prayer as thankfulness for the miracles that already surround us when we have eyes to see them.

This was the way Jesus taught the disciples to pray.

Not by the inch, but by the yard.

Not by the ounce, but by the pound.

They frequently withdrew from the crowds to be alone in prayer—not for a momentary ducking of the head, a hastily murmured word to the Father, but for hours of quiet communion, of throwing open the doors to their hearts and watching with hushed excitement for the rustle of the curtains when he crossed the threshold.

The time on the mountain when Jesus was transfigured was only the prelude. It was the picture to them of how it would be after the crucifixion. They were praying in the upper room when suddenly Jesus came and stood in their midst—without opening the door. Again and again it happened that way. The resurrection meant Jesus' freedom to come to them whenever he wished, wherever they were, in Jerusalem, in Galilee, or anywhere else in the world. They would never be alone, he told them. All they had to do to experience his presence was to pray.

Prayer is the attitude, the dimension, the posture, in which visitations come to us. That is a constant teaching of the Gospels.

"Oh," says the cynic, "that is only fantasy. It is pure, whole-cloth imagination."

Is it?

Perhaps you remember Shaw's St. Joan, in the play. Her political enemies accused her of not really hearing the voices of God that led her to her astounding victories in battle. "There are no voices," they said; "it is only your imagination."

"Of course," she replied. "That is the way the voices of God always come to us—in our imaginations."

When we have no imagination, we suppose that

the rational world, the world of our everyday percep-
tions, is the only world there is. When we do not
spend time in prayer and meditation, we miss the possibility of another world transcending this one, a
world of the spirit in which Christ comes to his fol-
lowers, a world in which resurrection is routine and
not extraordinary.

One of our problems with the disciples' praying is
that they said so little about it. Praying was so basic
and integral a part of their daily existence that they
neglected to underscore its importance to us. They
merely assumed that Christians everywhere would always pray. Therefore they passed no law saying *You
must pray daily* to be put on a placard and hung in every
Christian fellowship.

If anyone had said to the disciples, "You should
make a law about prayer for all the generations that
come after you," they would probably have laughed
and said, "Do we need to remind them to breathe?"

They didn't put it in bold print and underline it
for us, and now we tend to miss it entirely.

We fail, in the modern Church, to see how thor-
oughly prayer underlies the resurrection of Jesus, the
miracles of healing, and the whole world of Christian
belief. "I believe in God the Father Almighty, Maker
of heaven and earth, and in Jesus Christ, his only Son,
our Lord, who was conceived by the Holy Ghost, etc."
All those beliefs, but no "I believe in prayer, the waiting before God which opens my soul to all the irrational possibilities made visible in the lives of the
apostles." And as a consequence all the other things
we say we believe—God, Christ, resurrection, even the

forgiveness of sins—remain for many of us a sham and a puzzle and an impossibility.

Prayer has largely disappeared from our congregations, and with it the inner meaning of Christianity. It is foolish to preach on the resurrection of Jesus and try to convince modern audiences of its validity on the basis of arguments drawn from science or analogies drawn from nature. Only through prayer do we come to the meaning of resurrection.

Only through prayer.

There is no other way.

That is why I should have said to the girl who wrote asking about the resurrection, "You cannot understand it apart from the life of prayer."

When we pray, we enter into the mystery which Paul said lies at the heart of our faith. Jesus comes to us there. Resurrection meant his ability to do this. He was no longer limited by the world. He had overcome it. When two or three of us are gathered in prayer, he said, he comes into our midst. It is as we pray that we understand this, that we feel it happening.

It is as we generate the spirit of prayer that we begin to feel his presence among us. And we do not feel it more than we do because we have not prayed very much before coming together. Some have not prayed at all.

We do not understand this apart from prayer.

We do not really understand how resurrection is related to our own deaths until we pray. We know they are related, but we do not know how. And because we know they are related, we have often thought about the relationship—especially at funerals or whenever someone we love has died. But we do not understand the meaning of the resurrection of the dead until we pray.

When we truly pray, the character of death is altered. Then we feel God's spirit so certainly and powerfully in us that death no longer matters. It is no longer an enemy. We know that we are one with God, even as Christ was one with him, and we are one with Christ, and not even death is able to separate us, to alienate us, from the center of life.

I met a fine Christian couple from Colorado. They had lost their ten-year-old son in a freak canoeing accident.

The father had been attacked by a bee as they were floating downstream. Trying to ward off the bee, he swung his short paddle wildly around his head. The boy, who had risen from his seat to try to help the father, was struck in the ear by the flailing paddle and knocked overboard.

When he was recovered from the water, he was dead.

"I had a terrible time," the father said. "I felt so guilty I thought I would go crazy. I tried to blame God. 'Why the boy and not me?' I asked. I couldn't justify the senseless death of a child I loved so much. My wife fought it too. We both had a hard time. We fought it until we finally surrendered ourselves to God in prayer—and suddenly knew that we were not separated from our son. In Christ we are all one—we, the dead, the sick, the poor, the alienated, the enemy—we are all one in him. Now we see it is the only way to live."

The only way to live.

But we don't understand this without prayer. Prayer underlies everything.

✝ ✝ ✝

PRAYER

Lord, we have been so seldom in true prayer that some of us haven't understood any of this. Help us. Teach us to be quiet with you, to listen, to give thanks, to feel your presence. Become the center of our lives, Lord. Open us to all the wonderfully imaginative, irrational truth around us. Let us transcend the smallness of our everyday life and become one with you in Christ. We pray in his name. Amen.

Learning to pray means, above all, identifying oneself with every aspect of earthly existence.

Carlo Carretto
In Search of the Beyond

To pray is to take notice of the wonder, to regain a sense of the mystery that animates all beings, the divine margin in all attainments. Prayer is our humble answer to the inconceivable surprise of living.

Abraham J. Heschel
Man's Quest for God

I was with a friend, and since we were really too hungry to go on we asked whether there was anything they could give us. They said "We have half a cucumber." We looked at this cucumber and at each other and thought "Is that all God can give us?" Then my friend said "And now, let us say grace." I thought "Goodness, for a cucumber!" My friend was a better believer than I and more pious, so we read None together, and then we read a few more prayers, then we read the blessing of the food, and all the time I had difficulty detaching myself from the half cucumber, of which a quarter would be mine, and then we broke the cucumber and ate it. In all my life I haven't been so grateful to God for any amount or quantity of food. I ate it as one would eat sacred food. I ate it carefully, not to miss any moment of this rich delight of the fresh cucumber, and after we had finished I had no hesitation in saying, "And now, let us give thanks to the Lord," and we started again in gratitude.

Anthony Bloom
Beginning To Pray

Prayer and Human Sensitivity

It was the first meeting of a seminar on prayer. We were sitting around in a circle, talking about why we were there. Several persons, including some ministers, confessed that they needed help with their prayer lives. Others said they wished to learn more about prayer as a religious and psychological phenomenon. A few honest students admitted that it was the only easy course they could get at that particular hour. But there was one young man, a graduate student, whose reason for being there has always stuck in my mind.

"I'm into drugs," he said. "I like to get high. It raises my consciousness. I become more aware of everything around me. When I look into people's faces now, I can see behind the façades and feel what they are feeling."

He pointed to a notebook lying on a footstool in front of him.

"I can even get euphoric about that notebook," he said. "To most people, it is just a notebook. But I'm glad it's a notebook. I celebrate its place in the world. I'm grateful for existence and everything in it."

The young man's eyes were luminous with excitement. We were all listening intently to what he had to say.

"I like what drugs can do for me," he said. "But they scare me. I have seen what they can do to wreck your life. I'm here because I thought prayer might be a substitute for taking drugs. I'm hoping that prayer will make me more sensitive without the danger of drugs."

As I listened to the young man, I thought of something I had read recently in a book about Thomas Merton. It was written by a friend of Merton.

"When I remember my last visit with Thomas Merton," he said, "I see him standing in the forest, listening to the rain."[1]

Prayer made Merton one of the most sensitive men of our time. His years of quiet reflection in the little monastery of Gethsemani, in the hills of Kentucky, taught him to see and listen as few persons ever learn to see and listen. He would have understood about the notebook.

"Yes," I thought, "prayer will be all that you hope it will be, and more too. It is the very basis of human sensitivity."

Most of us, unfortunately, do not realize how much of life we are missing because we do not spend time each day in meditative prayer. Like Mr. Magoo, the nearsighted cartoon character who walks unknow-

---

1. David Steindl-Rast, "Man of Prayer," in Patrick Hart, ed., *Thomas Merton/Monk* (New York: Sheed and Ward, Inc. 1974), p. 79.

ingly through bank robberies, mass traffic accidents, and collapsing department stores, we think our lives are dull and routine, untouched by daily excitement.

"To set the mind on the Spirit," said Paul, "is life and peace."

Life and shalom.

Fullness.

But we take so little advantage of this. We live lives of drabness, without the technicolor and expanded vision of the Spirit. We don't see the beauty and excitement all around us.

Even non-Christian forms of meditation help people to be more alert to the world around them. I have long been fascinated by Zen Buddhism, with its emphasis on quietness and reflection, and the way Zen has contributed to the exquisiteness of Japanese art and culture.

Zen monks sit for hours at a time, clearing their minds of mundane thoughts, so that beautiful images can come in their places. There is no spot more lovely in all the world, I think, than a Zen meditation hall with its bare rooms and sliding doors that open onto graceful, immaculately groomed woods and gardens.

A Zen fountain is enchanting. It is nothing like the great, noisy fountains of Versailles or LaGranja. It is small and simple—a bamboo pipe, a hollowed rock with moss growing on it, and a little pool. The water trickles out gently and melodically, in harmony with the beauty of nature and the quiet mind.

A visit to a Zen monastery is one of the most restorative things in the world. It is not like going to Miami Beach or Waikiki or the Riviera. It is like going into the heart of stillness, where time and anxiety are obliterated.

It is like going into the heart of God.

Thomas Merton understood this. He saw a profound relationship between Zen meditation and Christian prayer. He too liked Zen monasteries. They reminded him of Gethsemani, and of other Cistercian monasteries sitting in beautiful isolation. He was on his way to the Orient, to visit the Zen monks, when he stopped by a monastery in California and was seen by a fellow monk standing in the forest listening to the rain.

The atmosphere of prayer in such a place, he told the monks, is very important.

"Enjoy this. Drink it all in," he said. "Everything, the redwood forests, the sea, the sky, the waves, the birds, the sea-lions. It is in all this that you will find your answers. Here is where everything connects."[2]

Merton liked the word "connection." It had a mysterious significance for him. It was one of his favorite theological terms. "Here is where everything connects."

Have you ever thought why the Jesus of the Gospels spent so much time alone, and why, when he spoke, his words were choicest images?

"Consider the lilies of the field, how they grow; they toil not, neither do they spin; and yet Solomon, in all his glory, was not arrayed as one of these."

---

2. *Ibid.*, p. 80.

"Behold the birds of the air, they neither sow nor reap nor gather into barns; and yet your heavenly Father feeds them."

Prayer was where everything connected for Jesus. It was where God and the world came together, in glorious fusion.

"I and the Father are one," he said.

Connected.

"You will be one with us too," he said to the disciples, "If you pray, if you abide in us."

And they were.

And you and I will be one with them too if we pray and abide in them, because prayer is where everything gets connected.

"To set the mind on the Spirit is life and fullness." Even in the most impossible settings.

Do you remember Jesus in the wilderness? He spent forty days and nights, at the beginning of his ministry, among the rocks and hills along the River Jordan. He prayed in that desolate landscape until, Scripture says, angels came and ministered to him— until the wilderness became a paradise!

We are quite good at just the opposite, aren't we? We can turn a paradise into a wilderness. Surrounded by the gifts of God—all we can eat and drink, a world of springing grass and budding flowers, people capable of love and laughter—we forget to wait upon God, to see him in all the gifts, and the gifts become meaningless to us. We look right through them without seeing them, because our minds are on other things. We become fidgety and anxious, and we pity ourselves and think what a hell life is—all because we do not meditate and see the miracles and give thanks for them.

One of my favorite stories is from Annie Dillard's book *Pilgrim at Tinker Creek*. Annie had rounded an outbuilding just in time to watch a mocking bird dive to the ground. It was a breathtaking experience. The bird seemed to step out on air, fold its wings, and plummet to the earth, thirty-two feet per second, accelerating as it fell. Then, a moment before impact, it opened its wings, revealing its band of white feathers, and stepped out on the grass as though it were getting off an escalator. Annie thought of the old philosophical conundrum about the tree that falls in the forest: If there is no one there to hear it, does it make a sound? What if she had not rounded that corner at precisely that moment and had missed the descent of the bird? Would there have been grace and beauty there, even if she had not seen it? Yes, she concluded, there would have been grace and beauty whether or not she had been there to witness them. "But," she said, "the least we can do is to try to be there."

The least we can do is to try to be there. Even in the worst circumstances of life. Perhaps *especially* in the worst circumstances.

There is a marvelous passage in Viktor Frankl's memoirs about his experience in a Nazi concentration camp. One evening at twilight, someone came rushing into the dull, squat little buildings where the prisoners lived and called to them to come outside. It had been raining, and the rain had stopped. The last rays of the setting sun were filling the gray, metallic skies with gorgeous color, and the puddles on the ground were all reflecting it. They stood there, those weary, starved little Jews, cut off from family and friends and culture, and stared at the beauty. After several minutes of moving silence, one prisoner said to another, "How beautiful the world could be!"

Even there, in those horrible surroundings where they were dying of disease and punishment and overwork, they could see the beauty and feel the presence of God.

You too can see the beauty and feel the presence—if you are connected. "To set the mind on the Spirit is life and fullness."

A friend of ours has a formula for getting connected.

Marge is a teacher. She works with retarded children. It is very demanding work, and often, by the end of the day, she is exhausted.

"Sometimes, when I am feeling depressed," she says, "I stop and think of something for which I am grateful, and I say, 'Thank you, Lord.' Then I think of another thing, and say, 'Thank you, Lord,' again. By the time I've thought of three or four things and said 'Thank you' for them, I've forgotten all about being depressed!"

When she gets connected again, the depression goes away.

Three or four years ago, I was speaking at a music conference on the campus of Wake Forest University in Winston-Salem, North Carolina. I told Marge's story during a Sunday morning worship service. The next day, as we were having breakfast in the cafeteria, a young woman came up and asked if she could share something with me.

She and her husband had come to the conference from Canada. On their way down, her husband had gone swimming and gotten an ear infection. On Sunday night, it had become much worse. He was in terrible pain and experiencing vertigo.

Frightened, the young woman had gone across the hall in their dormitory and awakened a neighbor. He drove the couple to the emergency ward at the hospital. An attendant there had given the poor man some pills but said he should return at 7 A.M., when a doctor would be there to treat his problem.

That was 3 A.M.

So the couple returned to their room in a strange dormitory to wait out the four hours until they could see a doctor.

"I was frantic," said the woman. "My husband was in terrible pain, and I didn't know what to do. But we remembered the story of Marge and how she said thank you. As I sat on the bed, cradling my husband's head against me, one of us began talking about things we were thankful for. We went back to things long before we ever knew each other. And, one by one, we recalled all the things in our lives for which we were thankful, and, each time, said 'Thank you, God' when we told them. It was amazing how the time went by. Then, at 7 o'clock, we went back to the hospital. The doctor put a drain in my husband's ear and gave him a sedative, and now he's sleeping like a baby. It was one of the most wonderful experiences of our lives."

Imagine—even in a situation like that. The importance of being connected—of being open to the Spirit and aware of the glory of life—even in a time of pain and suffering.

The instincts of our young friend at that seminar were correct. Prayer *does* make us more sensitive to things.

It makes us more sensitive to the beauty of the world around us.

It makes us more open and responsive to the people in our lives—to their needs and dreams and hopes.

And it makes us more deeply aware of our relationship to God, and to the way God has worked in our lives from the time we were born to the present moment.

And this, of course, gives us confidence in the way God will go on working in our lives as long as we live.

"To set the mind on the Spirit is life and fullness."

The important thing is to be connected.

‡ ‡ ‡

PRAYER

You have set us in a world of miracles, O God; forgive us for having missed them. Draw us to yourself in such a way that we become connected, and, becoming connected, find the true abundance of life. Through Jesus Christ our Lord. Amen.

Prayer is offering ourselves to God so that he may have a chance of doing in us what he is always wanting to do, but is prevented from doing by our going away before he has a chance to begin. It is God who prays to men, and men who do not listen to his prayers.

Louis Evely
Our Prayer

To know and to love God directly is to come to know what we are. All true Christian prayer also presupposes the further step, that there are things He will have from us and that some of our responses are true and authentic responses to His love and others are not. Prayer is an attempt to get ourselves into that active co-operation with God where we may discern what is authentic and be made ready to carry it out.

Douglas Steere
Prayer and Worship

Whoever wrestles with God in prayer puts his whole life at stake.

Jacques Ellul
Prayer and Modern Man

Prayer and the Will of God

Then Jesus came with them to a place called
Gethsemane, and said to the disciples, "Sit here
while I go and pray over there." And He took
with Him Peter and the two sons of Zebedee, and
He began to be sorrowful and deeply distressed.
Then He said to them, "My soul is exceedingly
sorrowful, even to death. Stay here and watch
with Me. And He went a little farther, fell on His
face, and prayed, saying, "O My Father, if it is
possible, let this cup pass from Me; nevertheless,
not as I will, but as You will."

—Matthew 26:36–39 (NKJV)

You may not have thought about it before, but there
are few passages in Scripture that haunt us more than
this one.

Consider what is happening in it: Jesus, strong,
vital, at the peak of a popular movement, yet knowing
that one of his disciples, a man he has taught and

trained for several years, has gone over to the other side and arranged to deliver him into the hands of the religious leaders, and that he therefore faces the probability of a trial and even death; having his last meal with his closest friends, then going with the most intimate of these to the rocky hillside known as the Mount of Olives to pray; telling the friends to pray with him, and going ahead a few yards and prostrating himself in the humblest of prayerful attitudes; and praying, even as the current of final events rushes around him like a mountain stream in the springtime, tugging him toward death and infamy while his human instincts cry to him to run, to flee the place as quickly as he can, "Father, not as I will, but as you will."

It is a magnificent picture, and the Western imagination has never been able to forget it.

"Not as I will, but as you will."

The most beautiful man the world has ever known—the truest genius of them all—and in the most dramatic moment of his life he underscored forever the importance of the divine will in personal events.

History, since then, has never been the same. Whole epochs have turned on this example.

St. Paul, who was an ardent lover of Hebrew culture, became a missionary to the Gentiles and changed the fate of Western Europe.

The emperor Constantine, who had opposed the Christian movement as "that insurrectionist rabble from Israel," saw a flaming sign in the sky and by a stroke of his royal pen translated Christianity into the most popular faith of the Mediterranean world.

Martin Luther, wrestling in his Germanic conscience with the distortions of faith in the medieval Church, struck out in a new direction that would change the face of the modern world; surely remembering the figure of his Lord in Gethsemane, he said, when commanded to recant and desist, "I cannot do otherwise."

Many of those who founded the original colonies of this country remained stubbornly on these shores despite disease and death and hardship because they were convinced that it was God's will for them to build a new nation for him.

The missionary impetus that has changed the face of country after country, in Asia, in Africa, in Latin America, has derived at least in part from the picture of Jesus in Gethsemane.

Yeats was right: two thousand years have been "stained by his blood."

But they have also been affected by this image of the man at prayer on the last night of his life, and by the words he prayed, "Not as I will, but as you will."

Think about it in your own life.

It does haunt your decision-making, doesn't it?

I have spent a lot of time with young people over the years, and find that most of them, even many who are outwardly very secular in their personalities, are concerned about finding God's will for their lives. They may not stop to ask if it is his will that they have a date for the movies, or that they take a trip to Europe, or that they enroll in a particular course in college. But when it comes to the really big issues in their lives—the occupations they should train for, where they should go to college, whom they should marry—they would seriously like to plan according to his will.

The same is true of their parents. They make most of their little decisions in a purely secular fashion. But when it comes to big matters such as "Am I working at the right job?" or "Should I take advantage of the big opportunity that has come my way?" or "What should I be doing about my children's future?" they often desire to have God's leadership.

"Not as I will, but as you will."

It has had enormous influence.

One major problem we all have, though, comes at the point of how we can know the will of God. It is one thing to be inclined to do his will; it is another thing to be able to know that will.

Haven't you heard people say, "I sincerely want to do what God wishes in this matter, and would, if I only knew what he wishes"?

Perhaps you have said it yourself.

"I am ready to commit myself to whatever God wills for me; my only problem is that I am not sure what he wills."

Sometimes, in the effort to discern his will, we do foolish things.

I knew a young ministerial student in the university who would stick a pin into the pages of his Bible, turn to the page where the pin fell, and then, without looking, point the pin to some part of the page. Next he would read the verse where the pin was and take that as God's message to him about the divine will for his life.

That has always seemed to me to be a rather risky business.

Suppose the pin landed on Leviticus 8:35? That verse says, "At the door of the tent of meeting you shall remain day and night for seven days, performing what the Lord has charged, lest you die; for so I am commanded."

Or what would one make of Deuteronomy 19:7, "Therefore I command you, you shall set apart three cities"? A governor might make sense of that, or a traveling salesman. But most of us would be quite puzzled by it.

And Proverbs 23:2 simply terrifies me: "Put a knife to your throat if you are a man given to appetite."

I heard the story of another young man who wanted divine guidance in choosing a wife. He loved two girls and could not decide which he should marry. So, one night when they were both having dinner with him in his home, he decided to test God's will by closing his eyes, turning around three times, and opening his eyes; whoever he was looking at would be the one God wished him to wed. He did it. He closed his eyes, turned around three times, opened them—and found himself staring into the face of an 83-year-old houseguest of his parents who was feeling ill and had come down in her bathrobe to get some Kaopectate from the kitchen!

I also read about yet another man who was facing a personal sacrifice he was not quite prepared to make and decided to resolve the matter by flipping a coin. "Heads," he said, "God doesn't want me to do it. Tails, he wants me to do it someday, but not now. If it stands on end, he wants me to do it now." And when he flipped the coin and it rolled around the floor and came to rest standing on end in a crack, he snatched up the coin, thrust it back in his pocket, and said, "Surely God wouldn't think very much of me if I fell for a cheap trick like that!"

These are humorous stories, but they reflect an anxiety we have all experienced at one time or another. How *does* one discover the will of God at particular moments of necessary choice?

Jesus didn't seem to have any doubt about what he was to do when he came out of Gethsemane. He knew God's will and he did it.

But how can we know? Sometimes we pray and pray about a matter, hoping to find God's will, and in the end we feel as confused as ever.

There is a reason for this.

Prayer is not a ouija board.

It does not function as an oracle for helping us to arrive at occasional difficult decisions.

That is simply not what prayer is about.

For that, we might as well flip a coin or close our eyes and turn around three times.

Prayer is a practice.

It is something one does constantly, from day to day, whether there are decisions to be made or not.

It is a way of life, a style of existence.

This is why Jesus was able to go into Gethsemane with the great weight of the moment upon him and come out refreshed, as though angels of God had ministered to him. He was not an occasional pray-er. He was a constant pray-er. Praying was as natural to him as eating or sleeping; in fact, many times in his life he had forgone eating and sleeping in order to pray.

We need to understand this. Busy as he was—there were times when it seemed the whole world was knocking at his door, wanting something from him—he spent hours and hours in prayerful meditation with God.

Sometimes he went up into the mountains to spend the night alone in prayer.

Sometimes he slipped off in a boat to pray. The disciples managed the sails and he was down in the hold, praying.

Sometimes, in the evening when it was cool, he went up on the rooftop to pray.

Sometimes he prayed walking along the dusty road, or sitting in a wheat field having his lunch.

Prayer was the very stuff of Jesus' life, and until we realize this, we cannot begin to understand what his prayer in Gethsemane was really like. He prayed without ceasing, to use Paul's phrase for it.

I have written in *Bread for the Wilderness, Wine for the Journey* about a friend of mine who is the wife of a dairy farmer.

This friend became aware of the need in her life for a time of special praying each day—a time when she would not be interrupted by the telephone or the children or the business of managing a dairy farm. When could she do it? She and her husband were already arising each morning at 4:30, long before daylight, and the day was filled with all kinds of activities.

There was only one thing she could do, she decided. She must rise at 4:00 instead of 4:30, and have her "appointment with God," as she called it, before anyone else got up.

It was hard. You can imagine how difficult it was, separating herself from the warm bedclothes an extra thirty minutes before daylight. But she did it, because she knew how important it would be to her.

And then one day, several weeks after she had begun this rugged discipline, she wrote this in her journal: "Just made a startling discovery! The time on my knees each morning is the *preparation* for prayer—the rest of the day then becomes the prayer!"

This is the way it was with Jesus. Prayer was so regular a practice with him—spending an hour here, a day there, a night here—that his whole life became a life of prayer.

Whatever he did was done in a spirit of prayer.

Whatever he said was said in a spirit of prayer.

Prayer informed everything about him.

When Jesus went into Gethsemane, then, it was not an isolated incident. He did not go there simply because the end was near and he knew it. The Gospel of Luke says it was their *custom*—Jesus' and the disciples'—to go there.

Prayer worked for Jesus that evening when he asked for the Father's will to be done because he was a *man of prayer*, not because of the importance of what he was facing.

That is a vital distinction. Jesus' whole way of life

prepared him for that moment. He didn't have any trouble discerning God's will for his life, because he opened his life to God every day that he lived. He listened to God. He waited on God.

What the hour in the garden of Gethsemane did was to revitalize his energies and regather his serenity for facing the awful ordeal coming upon him. We haven't understood the nature and meaning of prayer until we have understood this.

True prayer is never an attempt to manipulate God.

True prayer is lying open to God, the way a fallow field lies open to the warm spring rains, so that the gift of life may spring up there and grow to abundance.

True prayer isn't telling God anything. It isn't even necessarily having God tell you anything. It is just being there with God, mingling your presence with his, letting his being deepen yours, letting his voiceless voice communicate his innermost heart of love to your innermost heart of love.

We Westerners are so active. We expect everything to be based on activity and function and results. When we pray, we figure that we should be able to solve our problems. So we make a list of our problems—the way a functional Western mind would work—and we get on our knees and strive with God. We struggle with him to find the solutions we seek.

But prayer doesn't work this way. Prayer does not exist to give solutions. Prayer is simply spending time with God. The solutions come later, when the time spent with God has gotten our lives into order again.

41

Jesus in Gethsemane was not struggling with God to know his will. Jesus already knew God's will. Jesus was struggling with himself. He was facing the supreme test of his life, the surrendering of his life.

What Jesus did in Gethsemane was to open himself to God again, to reach back and lay hold on all those days and months and years of prayer experience he had already had, to let the strength and energy of all those times come to his aid now, to lay hold of the peace and inner power he had experienced so long as the gift of God.

I once had the opportunity of a visit with Archie Griffin, the great black football player who was the winner of the Heisman Trophy. We talked about the tremendous pressure on a star gridiron performer—all of those people watching every time he handles the ball. "You don't really think about it," said Archie. "It's all a matter of training. You train and you train and you train, and then when you get out there you just do whatever comes naturally. Sometimes you make a mistake, but most of the time you just flow with the game. The training carries you along."

This is the way it is with the will of God.

The training carries us along.

If we have been persons of constant prayer, finding God's will is seldom a great difficulty. We have become so steeped in his love, in his way, that it is almost impossible *not* to do his will.

I know this from my own experience. When my life of prayer and meditation is strong, I have no trouble discerning God's will for my life; anything I do is his will. It is when I have neglected to pray that I get into quandaries. My life becomes cluttered and disorderly, and then my mind becomes confused, so that I am not sure what the will of God is, or even if there is a will of God.

Matthew's account of Jesus' prayer in the garden is in chapter 26. Only one chapter before, in chapter 25, Matthew placed the parable of the talents. I suspect that he saw a definite relationship between the two passages. The story of the talents says very clearly what Jesus believed about the will of God.

> For it will be as when a man going on a journey called his servants and entrusted to them his property; to one he gave five talents, to another two, to another one, to each according to his ability. Then he went away. He who had received the five talents went at once and traded with them; and he made five talents more. So also, he who had the two talents made two talents more. But he who had received the one talent went and dug in the ground and hid his master's money.
>
> Now after a long time the master of those servants came and settled accounts with them. And he who had received the five talents came forward, bringing five talents more, saying, "Master, you delivered to me five talents; here I have made five talents more." His master said to him, "Well done, good and faithful servant; you have been faithful over a little, I will set you over much; enter into the joy of your master." And he also who had the two talents came forward, saying, "Master, you delivered to me two talents; here I have made two talents more." His master

said to him, "Well done, good and faithful servant; you have been faithful over a little, I will set you over much; enter into the joy of your master." He also who had received the one talent came forward, saying, "Master, I knew you to be a hard man, reaping where you did not sow, and gathering where you did not winnow; so I was afraid, and I went and hid your talent in the ground. Here you have what is yours." But his master answered him, "You wicked and slothful servant! You knew that I reap where I have not sowed, and gather where I have not winnowed? Then you ought to have invested my money with the bankers, and at my coming I should have received what was my own with interest. So take the talent from him, and give it to him who has the ten talents. For to everyone who has will more be given, and he will have abundance; but from him who has not, even what he has will be taken away. And cast the worthless servant into the outer darkness; there men will weep and gnash their teeth."

—Matthew 25:14–30

It is a deft story, isn't it?

The master is going on a trip and entrusts his treasure to three servants. Two of the servants are enterprising fellows. They go out and invest their funds in fast-rising stocks. Maybe they speculate on the international money market. The other is a dull fellow, pedestrian in every way. He is afraid of not being a faithful steward, of losing what has been entrusted to him, so he goes out at night and digs a hole and hides the money until the master returns. "There," he says, brushing the dirt off the money as he hands it back to the master, "you have what is yours—what you started with." But the master is incensed by this kind of stewardship! He gives the careful servant a tongue-lashing and casts him into outer darkness, and then gives a party for the two servants who doubled the money he gave them.

What is the story about? Obviously it is more than a simple morality tale about using our talents for God.

Consider the context of the entire twenty-fifth chapter of Matthew—all those stories about the scribes and Pharisees. Do you see?

Jesus told this story to say what was wrong with what passed for pious religion in his day. The scribes and the Pharisees were like the servant who had received a treasure—and then had put it in a safe place and stood guard over it until the master returned.

Jesus himself was the master! He had come and judged them—all their piety, all their praying on street corners, all their concern for the law of Moses.

But God didn't have possession of their imaginations! To them, the essence of true religion was to sit on the treasure, to guard it, to keep it safe.

To Jesus, it was living openly, dynamically, imaginatively.

It was living at the edge of adventure.

It was taking risks.

Do you see what this has to do with the life of

prayer? Prayer is a continuous placing of ourselves at God's disposal, a constant opening of ourselves to his presence.

If the scribes and Pharisees had prayed this way, they wouldn't have been like the prudent servant in the parable. They would have been growing, changing, taking risks all the time, so that the treasure God had entrusted to them would be blessing people all around them. If they had been eucharistic men the way Jesus was, living in perpetual thanksgiving to God for the miracles around them, then God's treasure would have been growing while they had the oversight of it.

But they were people who talked about the will of God in niggardly terms, and on special occasions, the way we do. They didn't live in constant openness to the will of God, as Jesus and his disciples did.

Contrast the disciples with the Pharisees. Let your mind run through the Book of Acts, remembering the imaginativeness, the openness, with which they lived.

Stephen preached a mighty sermon to the men who murdered him—so mighty that Paul would remember it later and it would be instrumental in his conversion.

Philip felt led to travel the desert road from Jerusalem to Gaza, and on the way met the Ethiopian eunuch in charge of the queen's treasury and witnessed to him and baptized him.

Ananias was praying when he had a vision and God sent him to lay hands on Saul of Tarsus, and Ananias did it, even though Saul had been breathing out fire and slaughter to the Christians.

Cornelius was praying in midafternoon when he had a vision that he should go to Simon Peter and urge him to come over and preach at Caesarea.

Peter was praying on the housetop about noon when he had a vision that Cornelius and his non-Jewish friends were as worthy of the Gospel as the Jews themselves.

Paul and Silas had been beaten and thrown into irons, but at midnight they were praying and singing praises to God when an earthquake destroyed the prison where they were confined.

Paul was at prayer when he felt the urging of God to travel to Rome, even in chains if need be, and preach the Gospel there.

You see?

They lived in prayer, and knowing the will of God was never a problem to them. Their imaginations were *aflame* with the will of God.

Oh, it is safer to be a Pharisee, of course.

They never got hurt.

Jesus was crucified, but the Pharisees were untouched.

The disciples were beaten, imprisoned, and thrown out of cities, while the Pharisees were safe at home in bed.

That is something to think about if you begin to get interested in prayer and the will of God. You can become radicalized pretty quickly if you begin to take prayer and the will of God seriously, if you make it an everyday business and not just an occasional, ouija-board kind of thing. It can make you a little crazy by the world's standards, so that you care about the kingdom of God and his little ones more than you care about wealth or reputation or personal ambition.

I know a businessman who took prayer seriously, and before his family knew what was happening, he had put half his wealth into a plan to benefit the employees in his factories.

I know a housewife who took it seriously, and it was only a year before she decided to become an ordained minister.

I know a doctor who took it seriously and left the comfortable university town where his clinic was to go to a hard little mountain town and become a doctor to the poor.

I know a dentist who took it seriously, and he and his family sold their two homes, their boat, their cars, and nearly everything else they owned and went to Africa to establish a dental clinic for black natives.

I know a well-to-do farmer from Illinois who took it seriously and rented out his farm so that he and his wife could go to Haiti as agricultural missionaries.

Maybe these people were just a little crazy. Or maybe they were a little more imaginative and creative than the people around them. Maybe they could see that life is more engaging and exciting when prayer and meditation open it up this way for you, when your life is on the line for God every day, when you don't have to worry about what God's will is for you in a particular matter because you are open and committed to him all the time anyway.

It is safer to be a Pharisee. But it is so much more thrilling and rewarding to be a Christian.

Ask any Christian who has ever lived as a Phari-see.

‡ ‡ ‡

PRAYER

Lord, not our will but yours. Not just now but all the time. In Jesus' name. Amen.

Is any one among you suffering? Let him pray. Is any cheerful? Let him sing praise. Is any among you sick? Let him call for the elders of the church, and let them pray over him, anointing him with oil in the name of the Lord; and the prayer of faith will save the sick man, and the Lord will raise him up; and if he has committed sins, he will be forgiven.

Therefore confess your sins to one another, and pray for one another, that you may be healed. The prayer of a righteous man has great power in its effects.

James 5:13–16 (RSV)

It would be a pity if scientists discovered persuasive evidence for the power of prayer at a very time when theologians were calling into question the value of the ancient Christian tradition of praying for the sick.

Francis MacNutt
Healing

I bandage, God heals.

Amboise Paré

In this ministry to men's bodies the Church has been so remiss and faithless that the therapy has been left to quasi-mystical cults which refuse the realism of fact, make healing almost an end in itself, and, what is worse, rob man of danger and heroism by denying the odds. These cults have their neglected truth, and cannot be answered by attack. The true rejoinder is in a Church which is realistically reconsecrated to the lost ministry of healing.

George A. Buttrick
Prayer

Prayer, Death, and Healing

Several years ago, one of my best friends in the ministry, a handsome, redheaded man with whom I attended seminary, died of melanoma. Harry was pastor of a Presbyterian church in Bucks County, Pennsylvania. Prior to seminary, however, he had been a Nazarene, and during his bout with cancer he reverted to his Nazarene background, especially as it concerned prayer and healing. God was going to heal him, Harry announced to everyone; he was not going to die. His faith was extraordinary. Even as his body visibly lost ground, his confidence seemed to ascend.

The local presbytery was embarrassed. Harry had come to their church only recently, and had not yet been installed. He demanded that the installation service go on as scheduled. They hesitated, not wishing to install a man who would soon be dead; yet they were afraid not to go through with it, lest Harry recover and they be shown to have had too little faith. So the service was held.

Harry was brought from the hospital. He stood for the charge, looking especially pale and gaunt in his great black robe. He announced again from the pulpit that God was going to heal him. After a reception in the church hall, he went back into the hospital.

Two or three weeks later, he died.

One man in his congregation, I learned, left the church. "If God wouldn't heal a man with a faith like that," he said, "then I don't believe there is a God."

I understood how the man felt. Nothing had ever tested my own faith or theology the way Harry's death did. When Harry's wife Mary Jo requested that I fly out to Columbus and preach at his funeral, I begged to be excused. I didn't feel that I could say anything. I needed time to think, time to feel, time to reexamine everything I believed about faith and prayer and death and healing.

Gradually, through the years, my thoughts have assumed some patterns. I say "assumed," because I have not tried to force them. The evidence has simply arranged itself.

I think some of my conclusions are important.

For one thing, I have become convinced that there are indeed miracles of healing through prayer.

I know that healing through prayer is a controversial subject in churches. The unsavory faith-healers we have seen in tent revivals and on our TV screens have given it a bad press.

But I also know that the healing ministry of Jesus and the early Church was such an intrinsic, inseparable part of what Christianity was about that we cannot talk honestly about the Gospel while ignoring it.

We would like to be able to tilt our agnostic, rationalist noses at the healing stories in the Scriptures and pretend they are not there. But when we leave the healing stories out of the New Testament, especially the Gospels and the Book of Acts, these books are as riddled with holes as if they were so many pieces of Swiss cheese.

If you doubt this, let me suggest an experiment.

Take an old Bible you no longer use. Turning to the Gospels, and using a razor blade, excise every section that recounts the story of a healing miracle.

Can you imagine the results?

Paper dolls!

You won't have more than fifty percent of the Gospel of Mark remaining, or fifty percent of the Book of Acts. Healing miracles were an inherent part of the New Testament faith. They represented the sovereignty of God over the world into which Christ's kingdom was coming.

Still, the world today is not as hospitable to the idea of faith healing as the world was then. With the rise of the universities and the development of modern science, we have become much more materialistic in our orientation. It is no longer easy to believe in what cannot be handled, measured, and studied in a laboratory. Even ministers and theologians have difficulty accepting the existence of miracles.

Dr. John Macquarrie, in his book *Twentieth Century Religious Thought*, deals with a hundred and fifty of the most prominent theologians of our time, and not one of them has shown any true concern for the way people's religious belief affects their mental life or physical health. One could hardly expect them to. They are scholars—scientists—and their empirical training often precludes their ready acceptance of miracles. Or, if they have experienced miracles, their training makes them reticent and they don't talk about them.

That is a large part of our problem. Because our view of reality is shaped by common experience, we need to hear about other people's miracles in order to believe in them ourselves. And, in the conspiracy of silence imposed by the scientific world view, most of us seldom share in the excitement of each other's miracles. We cease to believe in miracles because they are not given a prominent place in the way we talk about life. Sociologically speaking, blue-collar churches are more inclined than white-collar churches to give credence to miraculous occurrences. That is why my friend Harry, desperate to believe he would live, reverted to his Nazarene faith and friends; Presbyterians were not quite prepared to join him in the faith that he would be healed.

As a minister, I am privileged to hear many stories of people's healing miracles. It is hearing these stories that has convinced me, over the years, of the relationship between prayer and healing. All across this country, I have heard reports of miraculous healings.

I have told in *Bread for the Wilderness, Wine for the Journey* about a woman who came up to me following a lecture at Louisiana State University.

"I am five years old," she said.

I stared at her.

She laughed and explained.

Five years before, the doctors had told her that

she had only six months to live. Cancer had spread through her chest and lungs, and was beyond the operable stage. She made preparations to die. But her children were not ready for that. They belonged to a charismatic prayer group. Reluctantly, the woman was dragged along with them to a meeting. The group prayed for her. She felt different, and described the experience as if it were an electric shock passing through her body. She went back to the doctors for a checkup, and the cancer was in total remission.

She looked healthy, vigorous, and athletic. Her children stood there flanking her and smiling like angels.

I knew she was telling the truth. They were all too radiant for it to have been otherwise.

I heard a similar story in Texas from a woman whose husband had had melanoma, the kind of cancer that destroyed my friend Harry. The doctors had told him he hadn't long to live. He went to a pastor in Dallas whose church had been practicing meditative prayer. He began to pray that way for long periods every day. The others prayed for him. It had been three years, and the man was living a healthy, normal life.

A woman in Fort Lauderdale, Florida went to the hospital for surgery on bleeding ulcers. She had telephoned her minister and an elder of the church to meet her at the hospital to pray for her. The three of them went to the chapel and had prayer. She returned to her room and called her husband to bring some things she needed in the hospital.

When he arrived, she said, "I needed those things!"

"What for?" he said. "You're going home."

As he was coming into the hospital, he had run into her doctor. The doctor was amazed. He had just studied a series of X-rays taken only moments before, and the X-rays showed no sign of ulcers!

Receiving this news, the woman returned to the chapel to pray and give thanks to God. While she was there she encountered an older woman at prayer, and asked if she might share her good news with the woman. "I promised God to tell my story," she said.

The face of the older woman glowed with hope. She too was awaiting surgery.

"How long did it take you to get your room?" she asked.

"Two days," said the woman.

"I had to wait *ten* days," said the older woman. "Now I know why I had to wait so long—it was so that I could hear your story!"

She asked the woman who had been healed to pray with her. They prayed together for several minutes.

The next day, the woman who had been healed went back to the hospital with her husband to settle their bill. She asked her husband to wait for her a few minutes while she ran up to see how the older woman was. When she came back, she had amazing news. New X-rays showed that the older woman had also been healed of her problem. She was going home without having to have surgery!

Once, when my family and I were living in England, I had a phone call from my father. I knew something was wrong, because he never called. My mother was in the hospital with double pneumonia. She was very weak and not expected to live through the night.

"I think you'd better come home," my father said.

It was Friday. I telephoned the travel agency, but couldn't get a connecting transatlantic flight until Monday.

Separated from my mother's bedside by thousands of miles, there was nothing I could do for her except pray. I prayed all that day and long into the night.

The next day, a rare sunny day in January, I pulled my chair into the warmth coming through a large window, and sat alternately reading my Bible and praying. I was reading the Book of Acts, about all those demonstrations of the power of God in the lives of the apostles. And, as I prayed, I felt a strange peace come over me, as if everything was all right.

Later that day, when enough time had elapsed for it to be early morning in the United States, I telephoned my mother's doctor.

"It's a miracle," he said. "She turned the corner during the night."

There *are* miracles of healing through prayer.

But the power to heal is God's, not ours, and sometimes our prayers for healing are not answered.

That is what confuses us.

It is what bothered the man who left the church when Harry's prayers were not answered. It is what angered a man in my very first parish, when I was only a slip of a boy. The man never came to church, and people pointed out his house to me. They said his daughter had been very ill with pneumonia. He had prayed for her to get well, declaring in his prayers that if God permitted her to die he would never set foot in the church again. The girl died, and he didn't. I went to see him, but he wouldn't talk to me.

The point is, of course, that God is sovereign—not a bellhop.

God IS—what a statement! We should fall down and worship at the very thought of it. Sufficiently aware of his presence, we would not care whether we lived or died. The presence alone is enough. But, insufficiently aware of this, we expect God to exist in our behalf, to do what we want him to do. And, when we pray, we expect to be answered.

What we fail to understand is that prayer is not just asking God for things; it is submitting ourselves to him for his will to be done in our lives. It is yielding ourselves as channels for his power. And, when we have done that, we know that prayer has been effective even if our requests are denied.

God did not save Christ from the cross. Sometimes in our selfishness we forget that.

He did not answer Paul's fervent prayer that the thorn in Paul's side, whatever it was, be removed, even though Paul says he prayed for the removal three times.

But neither Christ nor Paul lost faith over this. Some people say that Christ did, because of that terrible line from the cross, "My God, my God, why hast thou forsaken me?" But those people do not realize that that line is actually the first line of Psalm 22, which is a psalm of victory, not a song of lamentation. Perhaps Christ spoke only the first line—we could understand an economy of speech under the circumstances—but he doubtless knew the entire psalm and said the words in a mood of triumph.

"My heart has turned to wax and melts within me," says the psalm; "my mouth is dry as a potsherd, and my tongue sticks to my jaw."

But the complaint turns into a paean of praise:

> Let all the ends of the earth remember and turn
>   again to the Lord;
> Let all the families of the nations bow down before
>   him.
> For kingly power belongs to the Lord, and dominion
>   over the nations is his.
> How can those buried in the earth do him homage,
>   how can those who go down to the grave bow
>   before him?
> But I shall live for his sake, my posterity shall serve
>   him.

And St. Paul, what did he do when the thorn was not removed? Did he pout and lose faith because his prayer was of no avail? Read his great letter to the Christians in Rome.

"We do not even know how we ought to pray," he says, "but through our inarticulate groans the Spirit is pleading for us, and God who searches our inmost being knows what the Spirit means, because he pleads for God's people in God's own way; and in everything, as we know, he cooperates for good with those who love God and are called according to his purpose" (Rom 8:26–27).

How did the old King James Version put it? "We know that all things work together for good to them who love God."

What we learn from attitudes like this is that God's healing has to do with a lot more than our bodies. Faith has to do with *inner* healing as well as outer healing. It has to do with surrendering ourselves to the will of God so that the rupture between God and ourselves can be healed.

And sometimes this inner healing, this healing of the rupture, is more important than outer healing.

One of the most important lessons I have ever learned about prayer and healing was given to me by a dear friend whose organs, especially her liver, were being ravaged by cancer. She had always been an open, inquisitive person, delving into one field of knowledge after another. When she discovered that she was very ill, she not only accepted chemotherapy for her condition but began also to investigate the matter of healing by prayer. She and her husband flew to Washington, D.C., where they had heard of a congregation of intelligent Christians that used their Sunday evenings to pray for the sick.

"What was it like?" I asked her when she returned.

"It was a remarkable experience," she said. She described all that had happened—how the names of those who were sick had been read at the altar by a laywoman while the congregation prayed. "The important thing," she said, "was the feeling of love you received, the sense that people truly care about you and whether your life is whole. They do not promise that prayer will make you well. That is not their complete goal. What they ask for is that you be whole, that you be healed from the inside out. They feel that even if you die you should die whole."

"I may not be healed," said my friend, "but I want to die the way they described it. I want to be whole when I die."

She was whole. She fought the cancer courageously. She gave her doctor permission to try every possible medicine, regardless of side effects, so that her experiences might be helpful to others. When she was in the hospital, too sick to sit up, she dragged herself down to the interns' meeting to talk to them about how they could minister to dying cancer victims. She gave her body to a black medical school, and her memorial service in a little Presbyterian church was a celebration of victory over death. Her husband and son led a procession, carrying a banner she had made: it showed white blood cells on a red field, with a large gold cross triumphant over the cells. At the conclusion of the service, her husband invited everyone to their home for an open house, because she had been famous for her open house parties. Everyone went and ate and laughed and talked. She had won, even in losing.

Do you see the point of that?

Death is no enemy when we are whole, when we feel that we are a part of the whole, when we are one with Christ in God.

The reason illness and death have become such

terrors in our culture is that we have become so fragmented and isolated in the culture. We live cut off from one another. We are not whole.

Have you ever read Margaret Craven's little novel *I Heard the Owl Call My Name*? It is about a wonderful tribe of Indians in the Canadian Northwest, and about a young priest named Mark Brian who is sent to live among them. The priest is dying, but doesn't know it. His bishop sends him to the Indian village because he believes it is the one place where Mark can learn to die. He is right. The people in the little village of Kingcome do not fear death, for they still live in simple relationship to one another. It is the outside world that is afraid of dying. When Mark Brian finally hears the owl call his name from the top of a tall spruce tree and knows he is going to die, he does not fear. The love of the tribe removes all fear. Wholeness—healing from the inside—banishes fear.

Will you understand if I say that is what Church is all about? It is about our being one in Christ and God. It is about a feeling of wholeness, of interrelatedness, that takes away our fear of death. It is about a healing so deep, so profound, that it removes our anxiety about mere external healing.

Sometimes this inner healing permits the outer healing to take place too; there is a mysterious relationship between the body and the mind, the body and the heart, and this is often possible. But it is not the most important thing.

The most important thing is to feel our wholeness in the body of Christ. Then we can say with the apostle, "Whether we live or whether we die, we are the Lord's."

‡ ‡ ‡

PRAYER

Lord, we are clever people and we know a great many things. But there are some things we admit we do not know as well as the early Christians knew them. We do not love as unselfishly as they did, and we do not understand healing the way they practiced it. Help us to submit ourselves to you in these matters and discover new depths in them. Through Jesus Christ our Lord. Amen.

Even the best of men, and perhaps especially they, when they return to a frank and undisguised self-awareness, confront themselves as naked, insufficient, disgruntled and malicious beings. They see their stubborn attachment to the lie in themselves, their disposition to infidelity, their fear of truth and of the risks it demands.

Thomas Merton
Contemplative Prayer

The only way to have at the same time a sensitive conscience and inner peace is the new orientation of life that comes from the knowledge of being forgiven by God and empowered for a new beginning.

Georgia Harkness
Prayer and the Common Life

Sometimes I consider myself there as a stone before a carver, whereof he is to make a statue; presenting myself thus before God, I desire Him to form His perfect image in my soul, and make me entirely like Himself.

Brother Lawrence
The Practice of the Presence of God

Prayer and Forgiveness

It is hard not to be sensitive to our critics, especially when they say things about us in public places. But it is easier to hear them when they write us delightful letters about ourselves, and then slip the criticism in as a wee bit of helpful advice. It was in the latter form that I received this word from a minister in a Western state: "I wonder how it is that you have had so little to say about prayer and forgiveness. I don't know if I am worse than other people, but I find that the need for forgiveness is one of the most crucial aspects of my praying."

Shortly afterward, I was studying the Gospel of Mark, and found myself puzzling over the passage in Mark 2:1–12 about the paralyzed man who was brought to Jesus by four friends and let down through a hole in the roof because they couldn't get through the crowds at the door.

"When Jesus saw their faith," says Mark—the

faith of the four friends—"he said to the paralytic, 'My son, your sins are forgiven.'"

That's what I was puzzling over.

Why should Jesus tell that poor man that his sins were forgiven? What kind of sinner could he have been anyway?

Maybe he was an unpleasant patient, as some of us are when we are ill or crippled. Or maybe he was a lusty old rogue, the kind who today would pinch the nurses in the hospital. Or perhaps he resented people around him who were not afflicted as he was.

But he certainly was not a notorious sinner, in his condition. He was not a highwayman who robbed people. He was not carrying on with another man's wife. He was not a greedy merchant in the market-place.

Why did the episode begin with Jesus' forgiving him? Surely *healing* was what he needed most.

Perhaps, I thought, Mark was setting up the story, arranging it to provoke a quarrel with the scribes who were present in the crowd. The scribes *did* get incensed about Jesus' forgiving the man. Maye they wouldn't have said anything about his healing him, if he had done only that. But they didn't like his forgiving him.

Then I remembered the minister's letter, and what he had said about praying for forgiveness.

I wondered. Were the two related?

Forgiveness.

Jesus said a lot about forgiveness.

He even set it smack in the middle of the prayer he taught his disciples: "Forgive our offenses, as we forgive those who are offensive to us."

Maybe it wasn't just an act with the scribes looking on. Maybe the paralyzed man needed the experience of forgiveness more than he needed anything else, and couldn't experience healing until he had felt it. That was plausible. People's physical problems are often engendered by psychological problems.

"Of course!" I thought. "The man's illness had something to do with his burdened, unforgiven spirit. It made sense for Jesus to forgive him, to set his heart at ease, before he lifted him up and gave him the use of his feet and legs again."

And it also made sense for me to give more reflection to the relationship between prayer and forgiveness.

Why did Jesus plant that bit about "Forgive us" so firmly in the middle of the only prayer he taught the disciples?

The world may be divided, for the purposes of talking about forgiveness, into two kinds of people.

The publicans, who know that they need forgiving.

And the Pharisees, who don't know it.

This fact runs through the Gospels, and finds its clearest statement in the little story of the publican and the Pharisee (Lk 18:9–14). Both men, the tax collector and the Pharisee, went up to pray in the temple. The Pharisee apparently went out of religious habit, and felt rather righteous about doing so. He even thanked God for the feeling of righteousness he had. He was glad not to come like the scurvy tax collector he had passed on the way in, who would not have been allowed to come past the outer court because of his dealings with non-Jews.

The tax collector, on the other hand, appears to have been driven to come to the temple by an acute awareness of his unclean status. Standing in the outer court, he beat his breast as a sign of contrition. All the time, he kept his eyes on the floor, not lifting them toward the inner courts, where the presence of God was supposed to dwell.

"God, have mercy on a sinner!" he kept saying over and over.

There they are.

The two types.

And Jesus obviously thought that the one on the outside was closer to the heart of God than the one on the inside.

What are we to make of that in our own cases?

Kierkegaard, you know, said that we are both publican and Pharisee, every one of us.

Sometimes we are more the publican.

Sometimes the Pharisee.

Let's think first about ourselves as publicans—as people aware of our offenses.

There is no doubt that prayer is an effective way of dealing with my sense of guilt. The case of the publican is proof of that.

When I know that I have failed in my relation to people around me—to my wife, to my children, to my friends—my most immediate need, even before I go to them, is to ask God's pardon. Somehow I know, as surely as the sun rises in the east, that my sin is against him.

When I have cheated—even in my thinking—it is God I have cheated.

When I have lied—even in my own mind—it is to him I have been false.

When I have been angry—again even in my own heart—it is with him I have shown displeasure.

So I go to him before I go anywhere else. My relationship to him must be repaired before I can repair it with anyone else.

You know what a wonderful relief to the heart this can be. It lifts a great weight off the soul, so that we relax and feel the tensions fall away. The whole body feels better. Life looks brighter again.

A friend of mine, a young man, has described for me the way he often approaches this prayer of confession.

He sits comfortably in his chair, he says, and imagines that he is a large burlap sack full of potatoes. The potatoes are all the things going on in his life—his loves, his resentments, his duties, his conflicts, his unkindnesses—all the things that are on his mind.

"When I am relaxed," he says, "they all spill out on the floor. Everything. All the desires, the fears, the frustrations, everything. Then God comes along and sorts them all out. He puts the good things back in the bag and takes the bad ones away with him. I feel renewed, unloaded, ready to go on again."

I resonate to that; don't you?

It is what I would like to have happen too, when I confess my sins to God.

One thing is certain: I can live creatively only when I have felt relief from the pressures of my guilt.

Guilt has a way of obstructing life—of keeping the flowers from growing. It is like a poison in the air of the soul.

I knew a man who had a quarrel with his wife. In his anger, he bolted out of the house, slammed the door, dove into his car, and went hurtling back out of the driveway. As the car raced backward, it ran over their two-year-old son who was playing behind a back wheel. The man realized it the minute he felt the tire strike something.

For months, the man could not forgive himself. He lost sleep, couldn't work, couldn't eat, couldn't laugh, couldn't give love or feel love.

His life became an endless round of remorse and self-hate.

At one point, he let his wife make an appointment with a psychiatrist. For weeks he sat in the psychiatrist's office, talking about all kinds of things, coming back always to his inability to accept what he had done to his little child. He didn't feel any better.

He became very religious, even to the point of neuroticism. He went to church constantly. Still he couldn't find peace.

Then one day, during a Good Friday service, he heard a minister talking about Jesus' sayings from the cross.

The words, "Father, forgive them, for they know not what they do" fell on his ears like rain on a parched land.

He sat there in the middle of the service and cried and cried.

When it was over, he went home feeling like a new person.

"I realized," he said afterward, "that if God could forgive the men who killed his Son, he could forgive me for what I had done to mine."

It is a blessed relief.

But I must admit that I am more concerned about the Pharisee in me than the publican.

About the part of me that doesn't recognize his offenses.

That part, I fear, is what is really obstructing my life.

I have not had many experiences near to the man's who ran over his child, and have never been bothered very much by a sense of guilt.

And that is precisely what frightens me.

Suppose I *have* had such experiences and simply fail to realize it. They could be poisoning my existence without my knowing it. That is really terrifying.

I think of one such experience that came to my attention.

One of my former students had a nervous breakdown. I received a letter from his wife saying he was in the hospital, and that he had had some trouble in the church where he was the minister—a dispute over leadership or something like that.

I was in a very busy flurry of engagements at the time, speaking in several places and trying to get ready for a trip overseas.

I wrote to say how sorry I was, that I would be

praying for my friend's recovery, that I knew it was hard on her and I was thinking about her too.

The young man recovered, moved to another state, took a position with a government institution, and resumed a rather frequent correspondence with me.

Then one day I received a bitter, seething letter from his wife. It was one of the vilest attacks I had ever read, denouncing me, my work, and her husband's attachment to me. It seemed so irrational, in fact, that I did not reply to it. I thought the woman must be losing her sanity.

Months later, when I was away from home, my wife received a phone call in the middle of the night. It was this former student, needing to talk to someone. He felt that he was on the verge of another breakdown. My wife talked with him for an hour. Then she heard the man's wife come into the room and discover what he was doing. She screamed and cursed at him, and told him to get away from the telephone. He tried to calm her, and apologized to my wife and hung up.

He did have to go back to the hospital, and I talked to him there after I returned home.

"Betty," he said, "has been angry with you ever since my first breakdown. She thought you should have come up to Jonesville and helped her to cope with my being in the hospital."

I was completely surprised by this. I had not at all read her letter as an appeal for help, only as a statement informing me that her husband entered the hos-

pital. I assumed that she had all the help she needed from friends in the area.

I subsequently wrote to the woman and explained this to her, but never received a reply.

How many times, I have since asked myself, have I failed other persons like this without realizing it?

How many students have I overlooked in times of deep personal need because they were shy and wouldn't say anything about it?

How many times have I been in my study, reading or working on a book, feeling good about what I was doing, and failed to address some moment of loneliness or remorse in the lives of my children?

How often have I neglected my wife when she really needed attention but had too much grace to say so in ways that would catch my eye?

For years, I have meditated on the tragic note of truth in an experience Herbert Farmer, the English theologian, told about in a book.

"I had been out all day," said a friend of Farmer's, "leading the busy life of a parish minister, calling on the sick, attending to various duties. I came back home about four in the afternoon, bone tired and desperate for some relief. I just had loosened my shoelaces and my vest, and had settled down before the fire with a cup of tea, when the doorbell rang.

"Two people stood there—a thin, tired looking woman in a frayed overcoat and very thick spectacles, indicating she was nearly blind, being led about by a quiet, worldly wise boy of twelve or thirteen. They were selling cottons.

"I'm afraid," he said, "I cut short a tale of domestic woes with a rather quick response that I needn't anything. 'Come away, mum,' said the boy, and led her out to the street again.

"For an instant at the gate, the boy looked back at me. I have never seen a look of purer hatred than glowed in his eyes at that moment. Suddenly I realized that the poison I had distilled into his heart in that thoughtless hour would remain with him for the rest of his life.

"Closing the door, I turned back inside the house, sick of heart, and fell on my knees to exclaim, 'God, have mercy!' It was all I could do."

It was exactly my own experience with Betty. In one thoughtless moment, I had poisoned her life forever.

And I probably do it to someone, somewhere, several times a year!

Perhaps this is why the minister who wrote said that seeking forgiveness is such an indispensable part of his praying. He realized that the web of human relationships is unspeakably complicated and fragile, that we must constantly beseech God to sensitize us and to absolve us where we have failed to be sensitive. Otherwise life would become intolerable.

I have spoken earlier of prayer's sensitizing us.

How important this is!

To wait before God, letting the images of faces come to us out of our subconscious

—the faces of old acquaintances we haven't seen in years—

—of people we work with—

—of family members, near and far—
—of public figures we have never met—
—faces in the newspaper, on television—
and to pray for these people, allowing God to draw our attention to present needs in their lives, to ways we can support and encourage them, to ways by which we can become channels of his presence and grace to them.

It is a good idea to keep a list of such persons, and to go through the list every day in one's prayers. No less erudite a Christian than C.S. Lewis kept such a list. The trouble was, he said, as he grew older, the list became so long! Yet he always hesitated to take any name off. There was nothing *wrong* with doing so, he thought; to say that one would pray for a certain person during a period of his or her life did not mean one had to do it for the rest of his life. Yet, when he came to cross out a name, he could never bring himself to do it on that *particular* day. "It somehow goes against the grain," he said; and he would leave it.

And, as for the people we don't know, but should pray for anyway, there is the example of the bishop of Liverpool, in England, who, when he and his assistant go to the altar each day for the sacrament and prayers, spreads out on the floor beneath them the pages of the daily paper, so that their eyes invariably fall upon the names of people who currently need the intercession of God's people.

And even then, when we have done all we can, it is still "God, have mercy," for there are those we shall have failed. It is inevitable.

"Forgive our offenses, as we forgive those who

have been offensive to us."

There is that last turn of the screw: forgiving others.

Not a very big thing, you say.

Easily managed.

But is it?

I thought I was easy-going, live and let live, bearing no grudges. Forgiving others was a way of life. I had practiced it for years.

Then I began to notice my dreams, my idle conversations.

I resented things my parents had done, or failed to do for me, when I was a boy.

I still had anxieties about conflicts with fellow students years ago.

With teachers when I was in grade school and high school.

With employers in places where I worked.

With colleagues.

They were all there—all those memories of hurts and words from years ago. Still there, after all those years.

And they were still eating—like acids.

"—as we forgive those who have been offensive to us."

It isn't easy.

It doesn't happen overnight.

Not even in a year.

We have to *keep* praying about it, keep turning over those past events, keep seeking forgiveness, for them and for ourselves. Not obsessively, compulsively, if they wish to lie dormant for weeks and months.

But whenever we sense any frustration arising from them. Whenever they interfere with healthy, wholesome relationships today. Whenever we *think* about them.

The secret, again, is to think about God's gift of love in Jesus.

That tortured figure on the cross.

The blood, the hurt, the suffering.

The loneliness.

And "Father, forgive them."

If *he* could do it—could pray for his enemies as his very breath burned in his lungs from what they had done to him—then *we* can do it.

And every time we do it we reaffirm the kingdom he preached, the community he died for.

We say, "Father, we're all part of one another. The good and the bad. The beautiful and the ugly. The friendly and the unfriendly. I accept that, and love it all equally, the way you do."

It is amazing how praying in the communion of saints can lighten our outlooks on life and help us to love even our enemies.

I have a friend who experienced a terrible youth.

His father died when he was five.

His mother became a prostitute, and then married a man who was cruel and short-tempered. Sometimes he beat the boy with a piece of barbed wire he kept in the house for that purpose.

When the boy was six years old, he went into a church building and dared God to show himself. When God didn't, he went outside, sat on the curb, and wept.

His stepfather ran a saloon and gambling house. When he was a teenager, the boy worked in the gambling house as a dealer. Then he had a fight with the stepfather and ran away, lied about his age, and got into the Navy.

Years later, after a life as a ne'er-do-well and a drifter, he married a kind Christian woman who was patient and good to him. He had a mystical experience and was called into the ministry. He came to school, though he was older than I was, and was one of my students.

I was astonished, when I heard his story, that he could speak of his early years without bitterness or regret.

"*Community*," he said. "I have a wonderful family in the Lord."

I have tried to pray with that knowledge, and my friend is right.

I become aware of the resurrected Christ.

Of the baptism of the Spirit.

Of the communion of saints in all the ages.

Peter.

Paul.

Matthias.

John.

The author of *The Cloud of Unknowing.*

The anonymous fellow who set the glass for my favorite window at Chartres Cathedral.

The nameless sextons who have swept and dusted the various churches I have visited in my lifetime.

The countless missionary families that have labored and died on foreign soil through the centuries.

The strong man who pastored me so gently when I was a lonely, romantic boy.

All my teachers.

How can I have enemies, when I think of this! I am part of all of them, and they are part of me.

And we are all in Christ.

And he is in God.

Forgiveness then becomes a great mystery—the mystery of the cross.

It wells up like a fountain of life.

I am drawn to it as a source of vitality.

It is the name of love.

When God says to me, "I love you," he is saying, "I forgive you."

When he says, "I forgive you," he is saying, "I love you."

And when I say "I forgive those who were my enemies," I am saying "I love you" to him.

✝ ✝ ✝

PRAYER

Forgive me, O God, for thinking I had no need of your forgiveness. That was crude of me; it was my own spirit speaking, and not yours. Let forgiveness become a creative force in my life, I pray, blessing all who come near me. Through Christ, who forgives and heals at the same time. Amen.

Actually, I have come to the monastery to find my place in the world, and if I fail to find this place in the world I will be wasting my time in the monastery.

Thomas Merton
No Man Is an Island

The true mystic is the one who constantly renews his mystical life in the actual field of politics. That is the first revolution modern mankind needs: men of prayer who are a prayer-force involved more closely than ever before in action and political combat. We have waited long enough. This age is peopled with still-born mystics. What this world needs is mystics who deepen their mysticism in contact with and in the melting-pot of what is newest in the realities of our age.

Jean-François Six
Prayer and Hope

I tried to pray, but every time I did I would think of somebody who needed help and I had to break it off to go help them. I could never get the hang of it.

Woman in Texas

Prayer and the World
of Action

Robert Pirsig made an interesting observation in *Zen and the Art of Motorcycle Maintenance*. When you're riding in a car, he said, you see everything through a frame, as if you were watching TV. When you're riding on a motorcycle the frame is gone. You're *in* the scene, not just observing it.

One of the things Pirsig was talking about was the difference between the active life and the passive life. Between being involved and merely looking on. Too many of us in modern life, he felt, have become passive human beings. We see everything going by— sometimes at bewildering speeds—but we are losing the ability to get involved.

Television may be partly responsible, because it provides vicarious action, a substitute for the real thing. Once, when we began to get bored with life, we went out and did something—visited someone, took a trip, started a new business, conquered another world.

Now we flip on a program and *imagine* we are doing something.

The danger, some people feel, is that we gradually lose the ability to *really* do something. Seeing everything through a frame becomes the only way we can relate to it.

It has long been the fear of some critics that prayer does the same thing—that it eventually becomes a substitute for action in the lives of those who pray.

We have to admit that the possibility exists.

You remember the story of the prosperous farmer who, in the course of his table blessing, was always sending up pious prayers for the poor, hungry family that lived down the road from him. One day his teenage son could stand the prayers no longer, and broke away from the table during one of them.

"What does this mean?" demanded the farmer.

"Father," said the boy, "if I had your corncrib I would answer your prayers myself!"

That is an illustration of how prayer can become a substitute for action.

We could all cite similar illustrations from our own lives—of praying for the poor but never giving a dollar of our own money to ease their poverty—of praying for an end to corruption in government but not caring enough to stop distorting the figures on our tax reports—of praying for peace but never writing our congressmen and women to complain of national policies that threaten the peace—of praying for the education of our children but never donating any time to help overworked teachers and overextended school systems—of praying for decent use of the media but never phoning the TV station to commend the programmer for showing something stunningly good—of praying for the evangelization of the world but never once sharing the good news with someone who obviously hasn't heard it in a meaningful way—of praying for love and understanding in our families but never giving love where it has not first been offered to us.

It is no wonder, is it, that praying has had a bad press in the world of action.

Words are cheap.

Praying is a habit.

Sometimes we don't really mean what we say.

We want God to do it all without its costing us anything.

We forget what praying cost our Lord.

The biblical view of prayer is that it leads directly to action. It may be communion of "the alone with the Alone," but it does not remain alone for very long. The idea that praying is for escapists, for people who want to avoid contact with the hard, cruel facts of life, is simply mistaken.

Take Jesus, for example. He began his ministry by going into the wilderness to pray. He was alone, quiet, away from the "world." But he ended his ministry by entering the turbulent city to face the evil men who were corrupting the simple faith of the people.

From the wilderness to the city. From peace to confrontation, bearing him relentlessly toward it as a river bears a leaf to the sea.

Nor were the years in between exempt from confrontation.

Again and again, the Master confirmed a singular rhythm in his life-style: from his hours of aloneness, when he worshiped the Father and sought the Father's will in his life, he returned invariably to a hectic ministry among the sick, the degenerate, and the victimized inhabitants of what was still, despite our romanticized view of it, a dark and barbaric land. The descent from the Mount of Transfiguration, when he was confronted by a demon-possessed boy, a distraught father, and the helpless disciples who had been unable to exorcise the demon, was only one instance. Actually his whole life, during those years when we have any information about it, was formed to the same pattern. Like a weaver's shuttle, his existence alternated between the quiet times of drawing strength, often purchased at the expense of his sleep, when others were in bed, and the crowded, exhausting career of a public ministry.

It was to be the same for his disciples, once they were put in charge.

They were all at prayer, the Book of Acts tells us, when the Holy Spirit broke over them like a tidal wave of fire, baptizing them with courage and the urgency of bearing witness to all that they had seen and heard during those extraordinary years with Jesus.

Later, Peter was at prayer when he had a remarkable vision confirming God's acceptance of the Gentiles; it was the strength of this vision that swept him up into the ministry to the Gentiles, in which he eventually lost his life at Rome.

Paul was similarly at his prayers when he felt compelled to go to Rome, even as a prisoner, in order to share his experience of the Gospel with those in the Imperial City.

We may safely assume, I think, that the same thing happened to Thomas, who legend tells us carried the banners of Christ into India, and to whomever it was that carried them into Northern Africa, and Spain, and Gaul, and the lands of the long shadows beyond the Alps.

Prayer, for these early giants of the faith, was not merely a means to personal integration, to self-understanding and consolation, as it is often viewed today; it was an embarking of the self upon dangerous voyages over uncharted seas and through dark, primeval woods, untracked by any previous traveler except the Savior himself, who, they always felt, had gone ahead of them and waited for them there, encouraging them when the obstacles were most severe.

Prayer was no retreat from the world of action. If anything, it plunged them into the very heart of that world. Instead of shielding them from trouble, it invited trouble; it courted trouble; it guaranteed trouble.

The reason is simple: prayer was where they learned the pattern of God's new world. Yielding themselves to the Uncreated, they began to see and to understand his design for creation.

They saw that he did not will suffering, but an end to suffering.

They saw that he did not want hate, but love.

They saw that he did not wish sickness, but health.

They saw that he did not want divisions among the peoples of the world, but unity.

And, from that point forward, they had to obey what St. Paul called "the heavenly vision."

It was as simple as that.

The Book of Revelation gives an example. The author—tradition said it was St. John—said that he was "in the Spirit on the Lord's day." That is, he was caught up in prayer. And, while he was in the Spirit, he saw "a new heaven and a new earth."

In this new heaven and earth, the Lord God was the center of everything. The very stars of the heavens orbited around his throne, and the voices of the angels swelled into a mighty chorus of praise, filling all the space there was. The river of Life—remember how important rivers were in the economy of mid-eastern nations!—flowed through the midst of everything. By this river stood the tree of Life, a remarkable plant whose leaves were for the healing of the nations. And there was to be no more sickness, no more death, and no more sorrow in this world. It was all to be joy, love, and praise. All life would be caught up in what it was created for—the enjoyment of God, forever and ever.

What man or woman, having seen a vision like that, could resist trying to change the real world, the only one we have, into the world of the vision?

I couldn't.

Could you?

There are those who insist that religion's business is not with the real world, the seemingly intractable world we live in.

You have met them, and I have too.

"Keep religion in the Church," they say. "It does not belong in the marketplace."

They do not see it as applicable to business, where profit is enthroned above everything else.

They do not think it belongs in the media, where entertainment is treated as the be-all and end-all—unless profit is still the king there, with entertainment as its court jester.

They do not see what it has to do with housing, or urban patterns, or race relations, or legislation, or national and international politics.

"These are not matters for religion," they say. "Stick to your praying and leave these things to us."

Which is precisely what a college president said to a friend of mine who was a chaplain in his university.

It was during the 1960's at a southern university. My friend had invited a black civil rights worker to speak in the university chapel service, and there was a furor in the press and on the campus. The local airport and bus terminal were swarming with out-of-town rednecks converging on the scene. The president, a good man but one who was harried by all the added pressures and the bursting of flashbulbs around him, said to my friend, "In the future, Father, please stick to your praying."

"It was praying," said my friend, "that got me into this."

He was right, of course.

Just as praying got Jesus into the crucifixion, and Peter into martyrdom, and Paul into prison.

Prayer and action belong together, you see. Each serves the other. To pray without acting is to miss the point of prayer, or never to arrive at its fullness, the surrender of the self to God as an act of love. To act without praying, on the other hand, is to act imprudently, unimaginatively, without the power of the Holy Spirit, so that the action becomes lost in a welter of confusion and misdirection.

We live in a world of enormous needs. They were always that way, of course, since time immemorial. Only now, with the advent of modern communication systems, we can get a better picture of them.

There is the need for food. Millions of people in the world go to bed at night with hunger pains in their stomachs. They eat grass and chips of wood and even stones to give their intestines something to keep busy with. In a recent documentary film of the devastating hurricane that struck the coast of India in late 1977, people were shown picking their way through a ruined field of barley, scratching up handfuls of barley grains, while only inches away were the rotting corpses of those who were killed in the floods.

Those of us who have high standards of living and enough food in the freezer to keep us for weeks or months are often forgetful of those who live so wretchedly. But there are more of them in the world than there are of us.

There is the problem of fuel. We begin to realize this when the prices of coal, oil, natural gas, and electricity rise at an alarming rate. But again we are well off compared to most people in the world. There is much less pleasure-driving in Europe, where gasoline prices are already triple and quadruple what they are in our country. In Afghanistan, peasant families may walk for as much as ten miles to gather a bundle of sticks sufficient to cook a single meal a day; wood has become so scarce that ecologists predict its exhaustion within a few years, leaving millions of persons without fuel for either heat or cooking; many will die by freezing in the wintertime. Nuclear power, which seems to be the most reasonable alternative source for the world of tomorrow, introduces problems of another character, especially with regard to the dangers of radiation and the possibility of terrorist or military activity.

Pollution, too, is a mounting problem. Despite our awareness of how rapidly we are despoiling the atmosphere, the water, and the land surface of our planet, we appear to be unable to set workable controls on our destructiveness. The world economies spin along at such a lurching pace that we fear to apply too much restraint, even for the sake of the earth that supports us. It is as if we had to choose between industrial chaos and a salvaged world, on one hand, and another fifty years of reckless exploitation on the other, with an irreparably damaged support system at the end of that time. Most governments, while preferring the first choice, seem to align themselves with the second, taking the long gamble that something will happen to change the picture before it is too late.

Greed, ambition, hate, and resentment, of course, play as large a part in world affairs as they ever have. The old battle between the haves and have-nots goes on with new actors taking the place of the old. People seem born to exploit one another, in business, in politics, in international affairs, even along religious lines. The children of the world, by the time they are three or four years old, have become snared in the same prejudices and immoralities that have governed their parents and grandparents before them.

What is the answer to all of this?

We know God's answer.

> Arise, shine; for your light has come,
>   and the glory of the Lord has risen upon you.
> For behold, darkness shall cover the earth,
>   and thick darkness the peoples;
> But the Lord will arise upon you,
>   and his glory will be seen upon you.
> And nations shall come to your light,
>   and kings to the brightness of your rising.

—Isaiah 60:1–3

The early Christians, who were people of prayer and devotion, heard this word and responded. Their lives were transformed by it. They rose above the greedy, grubby culture of their time, to become guiding lights of morality, courage, and unselfishness.

Not even centuries of darkness and indifference have managed to completely extinguish those lights; somehow they shine on in the gloom, casting at least a faint glow of hope on our own horizon.

But it is left to us, who have such a clear picture of our world's sore needs and problems, to turn on the lights in our time. The world will not be saved by their light, but by ours.

Now, at the end of the twentieth century, the world will not come under the power of Christ through their lives, but through ours.

We cannot fold our hands, retreat from the conflict, and expect God to redeem everything. If we have learned anything, we have learned this: that he acts in every age through his people, and only through his people. That is the lesson of history. It is the story of the New Testament.

If we had been praying as we should, we would not need to hear such things. We would know them instinctively, because we would already be caught up in changing the world.

The thing about prayer is that it is the way we can turn the unlimited resources of God into saving the world around us.

When we truly pray, when we open ourselves to God without reservation, it is like turning a valve in the largest dam in the world, so that the tremendous power that has been embraced behind the dam is suddenly released through the aperture the valve was controlling, and goes shooting forth with incredible energy into the valley below.

We are not the power.

We do not have to be powerful in ourselves.

All we have to do is to be an opening, and let God do the rest.

I have a friend who became an opening. In his praying, he kept seeing all those little villages in India where the people were poor and starving because there was no water for irrigation or for raising cattle.

When he really prayed, so that he became an opening instead of a closure, he saw what he could do.

He went around to churches and business people and whomever he could tell his story to, and asked for money to dig wells all over India.

"For every thousand dollars I can get together," he said, "I can sink a new well. One well, in a small village, will bring new life and hope to all the people there. They can have cows. The children will not starve any longer. They will have a chance for the future."

He was as grateful for a ten dollar gift as he was for a hundred or a thousand.

Soon he had collected thousands of dollars, and he went to India. Everywhere he went, he brought in the government agricultural service to determine where the best place for a well would be, and then he paid for a well to be dug. Now, in dozens of places all over India, there are villages where people no longer have to walk miles with pails to get water for their cooking and drinking purposes, but can draw water in their own locales.They can raise grain and vegetables and cattle. There is milk for the babies.

All because my friend prayed and became an opening for God.

Do you see?

It is what we must do for the world.

Hundreds of us, thousands of us, must become openings for God. We must perforate the barrier between his resources and our world's needs, so that he is able to pour through into our world with all his healing power.

In the end, it all has to do with love.
God's love for the world.
Our love for the world.
Our opening ourselves to God, so that his love can reach the world through us.
This is what it means to become Christians, for it is what Christ did. By praying constantly, he became the perfect opening. God came into the world through him.
We call that the good news.
But it is only part of the good news.
The other part is: God comes into the world through you too.

† † †

PRAYER

Here am I, Lord. Make me an opening. Amen.